LYNDA RADLEY

Lynda Radley is a playwright, storyteller and dramaturg. Previous work includes *The Mother Load*, *Christmas Tales* (Royal Lyceum Theatre, Edinburgh), *Fourteen Voices From The Bloodied Field* (Abbey Theatre), *The Maid's Room, There Is Someone Who Hates Us* (National Theatre of Scotland), *Ligach And The Salmon* (Pitlochry Festival Theatre), *Happier Or Better?* (Royal Conservatoire of Scotland), *The Interference* (Pepperdine Scotland), *Berlin Love Tour, The Heights, The Art Of Swimming, Soap!*, *Integrity* (Playgroup) *Futureproof* (Traverse Theatre/Dundee Rep), and *Birds And Other Things I Am Afraid Of* (The Arches/Poorboy).

Radio work includes *Our Sentence* (BBC Radio Scotland) and *An Irish Airman Forsees His Death* (BBC Radio 4). Lynda received Scotsman Fringe First Awards for *Futureproof* and *The Interference*; the latter was also shortlisted for the Amnesty International Freedom of Expression Award. Her play *DORM* was shortlisted for the Bruntwood Prize for Playwriting. She is a board member of Playwrights' Studio Scotland.

Other Titles in this Series

Lynda Radley

FUTUREPROOF

NICK HERN BOOKS

London

www.nickhernbooks.co.uk

A Nick Hern Book

Futureproof first published in Great Britain as a paperback original in 2011 by Nick Hern Books Limited, The Glasshouse, 49a Goldhawk Road, London W12 8QP, in association with the Traverse Theatre, Edinburgh

Futureproof copyright © 2011, 2021 Lynda Radley

Reprinted with revisions in 2021

Lynda Radley has asserted her right to be identified as the author of this work

Cover photo: Euan Myles
Cover design: Ned Hoste, 2H

Typeset by Nick Hern Books, London
Printed and bound in Great Britain by CLE Print Group Ltd, St Ives, Cambs PE27 3LE

A CIP catalogue record for this book is available from the British Library

ISBN 978 1 84842 213 1

Woodland CARBON
www.woodlandcarbon.co.uk
NICK HERN BOOKS
Printed on Carbon Captured paper

Futureproof was first produced by Dundee Rep Ensemble and the Traverse Theatre Company, and performed at the Dundee Rep Theatre on 3 August 2011 before transferring to the Traverse, Edinburgh, as part of the Edinburgh Festival Fringe. The cast and creative team was as follows:

RILEY	John Buick
GEORGE/GEORGINA	Lesley Hart
MARKETA	Irene Macdougall
TINY	Robert Paterson
LILLIE	Ashley Smith
MILLIE	Nicola Roy
SERENA	Natalie Wallace

Director	Dominic Hill
Designer	Colin Richmond
Lighting Designer	Guy Hoare
Composer	John Harris
Movement Directors	Janet Smith and Sally Owen
Audio Visual Designer	Kim Beveridge
Company Stage Manager	Nils Den Hertog
Deputy Stage Manager	Richard Lodge
Assistant Stage Managers	Lesley Neilson and Lauren Simmonds
Wardrobe Supervisor	Phyllis Byrne
Wardrobe Assistants	Susan Doyle and Enza Dormizzi
Wardrobe Assistant/Dresser	Cleo McCabe
Cutter	Liz McCaffery
Prosthetics	Morag McLain
Wigs	Annemarie O'Neil

The revised version of the play published here was created for an Irish tour of *Futureproof* in 2017, directed by Tom Creed, and produced by the Everyman Palace Theatre, Cork, and Project Arts Centre, Dublin, with funding from the Arts Council of Ireland.

Author's Thanks

This play was written with the support of a Creative Scotland (formerly Scottish Arts Council) Writer's Bursary.

Sincere thanks to Dominic, Katherine, and all at the Traverse; Julie Ellen, Iain Finlay MacLeod, and all at the Playwrights' Studio Scotland; Philip Howard, John Fairleigh and all at the Stewart Parker Trust; Frances Poet and all at the National Theatre of Scotland New Work Department; and Martin Cloonan. Thank you to Tom Creed for his notes on the updated 2017 Irish tour edition of the the text. Thanks also to my brother Bryan and my mother Mary for their support. Most of all, thank you to Michael John McCarthy for being an insightful dramaturg as well as a wonderful husband.

Lynda Radley

For Dad

Terry Radley (1953–2008)

Characters

ROBERT RILEY, *owner and caller of Riley's Odditorium*
TINY, *a fat man*
THE COUNTESS MARKETA, *an armless bearded lady*
LILLIE *and* MILLIE, *conjoined twins joined at the pelvis*
GEORGE/GEORGINA, *an intersex person*
SERENA, *a mermaid*

Note on Costume

Due to the nature of Riley's show, George/Georgina should
wear a 'half-and-half' costume; where on one side of the body
the hair is long, skin pale and clothes feminine, and on the other
side the hair is short, skin tanned and clothes masculine.

Note on the Text

Serena does not speak and it is painful for her when she walks.
She communicates through gestures that can be universally
understood. As the play progresses she makes sounds or writes.
When she eventually speaks it is with great difficulty, at least to
begin with.

One

A patch of wasteground outside a small town. No time in particular.

The Odditorium and characters arrive. The characters begin to unpack.

TINY. I'm starving.
  What's for tea?

LILLIE. I think there's a little horse meat left.

TINY. Not horse.
  I've been dreaming about poor Blackie.
  I can still see his big brown eyes.

MILLIE. I could make you another sugar sandwich.
  You like those.

TINY. Say a prayer for the teeth I have left.

MARKETA. It's not just him who is hungry, you know.

  GEORGE/GEORGINA *starts lighting the stove.*

RILEY. I am aware. Quite aware.
  So why don't you all continue to set things up here,
  while I go into town and see if I can't fatten the feast.

TINY. Feast! Ha!

MARKETA. No more bread and cheese, huh.
  Try and get some fruit or something.

RILEY. For you, Countess, I'll do my best.
  (*To* LILLIE *and* MILLIE.) And in the meantime…

LILLIE *and* MILLIE. A snack for Tiny.

TINY. Thanks, Boss.

GEORGE/GEORGINA. Don't be long.

RILEY *leaves.*

TINY *finds his bag, takes out a folding stool and sits down.*

LILLIE *and* MILLIE *gather what they need.*

MARKETA, SERENA *and* GEORGE/GEORGINA *silently set up the camp.*

TINY *very deliberately and ceremoniously unpacks his bag. It contains a folding table, silverware and dishes. When he has done this, he takes his place; napkin tucked in, cutlery in hand, ready to be fed. He waits, motionless.*

LILLIE *and* MILLIE *are preparing food, their four hands dancing. They work as one and speak quietly to each other.*

LILLIE *sighs.*

MILLIE. You're sighing, sister.

LILLIE. Am I?

Pass the –

MILLIE *hands her a knife.*

It's only that here we are again trying to make something of nothing.

No doubt they'll all complain.

MILLIE. No doubt.

LILLIE. Once I've eaten something…

MILLIE. Yes, once we eat something, however small…

LILLIE.…however small things will seem better.

LILLIE *passes the sugar to her sister but does not catch her eye. They continue to work.*

Pause.

MILLIE. You can have this evening.
If you like.

LILLIE. No.
We agreed.
You shouldn't.

MILLIE. As a treat.
I don't mind.

LILLIE. Well… if you're sure.

MILLIE. Sure I'm sure.

LILLIE *kisses her sister.* MILLIE *smiles.*

They resume working.

LILLIE. To bed after dinner then.

MILLIE. Bed is your choice?

LILLIE. I'm tired.

MILLIE. You wouldn't rather sew or look at magazines…
Or take a walk?

LILLIE. I have a headache.
And we've been walking all day.

Beat.

MILLIE. To bed after dinner.
I'll read.

LILLIE. But keep the lamp low.

MILLIE. Yes.

Beat.

Perhaps a walk tomorrow…

They work on.

SERENA *exits. Nobody notices.*

GEORGE/GEORGINA *has made tea and brings them both
a cup.*

GEORGE/GEORGINA. Ladies.

LILLIE. Thanks, George/Georgina.

MILLIE. Yes, thanks, G.
  You're very kind.

GEORGE/GEORGINA. Welcome, Millie.

  Miss Lillie.

MARKETA. Can I get one of those?

TINY. And me.
  I'm parched.

GEORGE/GEORGINA. Yes, yes.

  Coming, coming.

  LILLIE *sips her tea and sighs again*.

MILLIE. It must be a bad headache.

LILLIE. Well, given the way things are…

  Beat.

MILLIE. Still,
  there's more to your sighing than that, though.
  But of course you needn't say.

  LILLIE *puts down her knife*.

LILLIE. We *do* have two heads, you know!

MILLIE. I can't help sensing things.

LILLIE. We at least have that.

  Pause.

  …I'm thinking about that man.
  One town back.

MILLIE. The one who asked to see us in our scanties?

LILLIE. No!

  They giggle.

  No… the one who came every day and stood at the back.

MILLIE. Him.

Beat.

I think he liked you, Lil.

LILLIE. How do you know?

MILLIE. He would close one eye when he looked.

They return to their chores and work in silence.

TINY. I'm ruined.

MARKETA. We pushed as well, you know.

TINY. It's not the same.
Think of the cost!
For me.
The cost of me!

MARKETA. Don't worry.
You're still fat.

TINY. Yes, but for how long?
And how fat?
Fat enough?
Stunningly fat?
Gloriously fat?
Or just slightly larger than them?

LILLE *and* MILLIE *bring* TINY *his sandwich.* TINY
swallows contemplatively.

MARKETA. Where's what's-her-name?

TINY. Who?
Fish-face?

MARKETA *laughs.*

MARKETA. Shh! She's harmless.

TINY. Harmless?
Holding her breath, wearing a tail.
Pure pretence!
It makes me heartsore to think we've stooped so low.

MARKETA. I'm not a real countess and you're not the fattest man in the world but we don't tell them that.

TINY. It's not about them.
It's about what *we* know to be true and there's a code to that.
And that code's been round longer than you've been alive.
First: reals, like you, on top.
Then mades, like me, following close behind.
Then gaffs; fakers who give us all a bad name, but at least try to appear the genuine oddity.
Lastly novelty acts,
like her,
firmly at the bottom of the barrel.
Miss Serena puts it on.

Beat.

She doesn't *live it* like we do.
Time was that was a sin in the shows.
Time was when Mr Riley would have had nothing to do with it.

MARKETA. It's not her act, but her silence that gets to me. It's…

TINY. Disarming?

MARKETA. Ha! The act is pretty though.
They like it.
She's keeping us in bread and cheese at least.

TINY *(pointed)*. Novelties are for children and the simple-minded.

MARKETA. Well, at least it's something.
What's the point of standing up there if there is none to look?
And none to pay.

They consider this. TINY *has finished his meal.* GEORGE/ GEORGINA *brings* TINY *and* MARKETA *their teas.*

Thanks.
You're a… darling.
What do you think, George/Georgina?
Is Tiny fat enough?

GEORGE/GEORGINA (*considers*). Yes.
    Still sufficiently fat.

TINY. Sufficiently?
    Sufficiently?!

    MARKETA *laughs*.

GEORGE/GEORGINA. 'Sides, Mr Riley says:
    'It's not the act.
    It's the tale that gets told.'

MARKETA. Well, he would think that, wouldn't he?

TINY. Look, this is serious.

    (*To* GEORGE/GEORGINA.) What would *you* do if I could
    make you one thing or the other?

    GEORGE/GEORGINA *doesn't know how to respond*.

    (*Interrupting*.) Or you, Marketa, if I shaved off your beard?
    Or grew you some arms?

MARKETA. Either way *I'd* still have an act, eh?
    That's the beauty of being two-fold.

TINY. And if I were to do both?

MARKETA. I would make the most of it.
    Probably.
    Find a nice rich man and have babies.
    Something like that.

TINY. Well, that's hardly out of the question even now.
    You've never been short of admirers.
    Regardless.

MARKETA. Yes.
    Imagine!
    Regardless.

    Silence.

    GEORGE/GEORGINA *wanders away from them and sits by
    the stove*.

You. Worrying about shrinking down the billing when there might not be a billing at all.

TINY. Perhaps a nap will put me in a better mood…

MARKETA. Yes, sleep it off, fatso.
Maybe he'll bring back a pie.

TINY *falls asleep*.

Two

RILEY *returns to the camp. He is bleeding from the forehead and his trousers are muddy.*

MARKETA. What happened?

GEORGE/GEORGINA. Should pack? Should run?

RILEY. It's alright, it's alright!
I slipped in the ditch.
It's nothing.

GEORGE/GEORGINA. Not nothing.
You're bleeding.

RILEY. I'm fine.

GEORGE/GEORGINA *tries to place a hanky on the wound.*
RILEY *takes it and holds it there himself.*

No need to worry.

Beat.

GEORGE/GEORGINA. You're sure?

RILEY. False alarm.
I'm fine.
We're fine.

Beat.

MARKETA. What's it like?

RILEY. Small town.
Village really.
Should be alright.

MILLIE. That's a relief.

He hands LILLIE *a cloth sack. She peers inside.*

LILLIE. This is 'fattening the feast'?

GEORGE/GEORGINA. Lillie!

RILEY. I'm sure you will manage in style as always, Miss Lillie.
Important to keep spirits up.
I thought we agreed.

GEORGE/GEORGINA. Any money to be seen?

RILEY. Could see a few pockets left wide open, ripe for
picking.

A less moral man than myself might have had a field day.
But then we couldn't stay.
And I think we will, for a while.

Beat.

Now, don't worry about food for me, I met a business
acquaintance in town and he very kindly…

SERENA *enters carrying a large fish. She places it before
the twins.*

LILLIE. A.

MILLIE. Fish.

They throw their four arms around SERENA, *who is both
surprised and delighted and hugs them back.*

(*To* GEORGE/GEORGINA.) Look, G! A fish.

RILEY. Where did you get that from?

SERENA (*gestures*). 'Where d'you think?'

LILLIE. Do we have to tell Tiny?

MARKETA. Probably smells it already…

LILLIE *takes* SERENA *by the hand and she, the twins and* MARKETA *begin to prepare the fish. They leave* TINY *sleeping.*

GEORGE/GEORGINA *tends to* RILEY*'s bleeding forehead, apart.*

RILEY. She's a bit of an obscurity that one.

GEORGE/GEORGINA. More than a bit, Boss.

RILEY. Team player though, it has to be said.
    We should send her out with a pole more often.

Beat.

GEORGE/GEORGINA. Who did this?

RILEY. Nobody.
    I told you.
    I slipped in the ditch.
    I was absorbed in how best to solve our current cash-flow problems and I lost my footing.

Pause.

Some young men from the town.
Called me a carny and threw a few stones,
with surprising accuracy.

Beat.

They laughed when I fell over.

Beat.

Doesn't matter.
I'd rather not dwell.

Beat.

Made off with a bag of apples.
That's the worst part.

GEORGE/GEORGINA. Still,
    you want to stay?

RILEY. We can't run away every time someone throws stones.

Beat.

How was morale in my absence?

GEORGE/GEORGINA. Alright.
The twins needling each other about something.
Tiny worried about the breach of code that Miss Serena's act signifies.

RILEY. The fish will fix that.

GEORGE/GEORGINA. For a while.

Beat.

And also about… *losing his figure.*

RILEY. Ah.

GEORGE/GEORGINA. Even asked what Marketa would do if someone made her unstrange.
Or George/Georgina… if… could be one thing or the other.

RILEY. And what did you say?

GEORGE/GEORGINA. Can't be done, can it.
'Sides
Tiny is still within critical mass.
He's prone to exaggeration.

RILEY. The fat man's curse.

Beat.

You must have thought about it though?
How it would be? To be one way?

GEORGE/GEORGINA. When the male… parts became…
apparent.
Twelve years old.
Would have given anything.
Even tried pretending.
Always found out though.
One way or another.
And people can never forgive.

Men crack a rib or two.
Women go silent.
Even mothers.
Though there's nothing can be done.

RILEY (*looks at* GEORGE/GEORGINA). You as a girl.
A girl alone.

GEORGE/GEORGINA. Examined like livestock by thick-
fingered men.
Sized up in terms of hips and acreage. And can she graft?
And can she milk a cow?
Married off to the highest bidder.
All a lottery.
(*Lying*.) Better to be looked at and paid at least.
Or, well,
paid in theory anyway.

RILEY *grimaces, stung by the disinfectant*.

Sorry.
Was thinking, Boss, that maybe we need to clean up our act.

RILEY. I run a clean house.
A clean house.
I pride myself on –

GEORGE/GEORGINA. No, not that. But...
To change how they feel about it.
Make it seem less like a sideshow and more like a show.
Something where they don't mind who sees them there.
And not just places like this, but in the big towns too.
When they can bring themselves to look, they like it
or at least, it stirs them...

Pause.

Sorry, Boss.
Don't mean to overstep...

RILEY. No, you're right.
You're right.

Beat.

Maybe Tiny has a point after all, eh?

GEORGE/GEORGINA. Tiny?
It was only hunger talking.

RILEY. I don't know.
It's their shame that smarts yet we're the ones who feel it.
If there was a way to solve that...

Beat.

Have you had anything to eat?

GEORGE/GEORGINA. No.
Not yet.

RILEY *begins to move away.*

RILEY. Well, why don't you go and get something while you
still have the chance.
Go on.
I've a little thinking I'd like to get done before bedtime.

GEORGE/GEORGINA *leaves.*

Three

The group in preparation for a show:

MARKETA *dressed in finery, painting with her mouth.*

LILLIE *and* MILLIE *fixing their costume and practising
dance steps.*

SERENA *setting up her bathtub and mermaid's tail.*

GEORGE/GEORGINA *setting up dumb-bells on the masculine
side of a performance podium and sewing on the feminine side.*

TINY *enters, out of breath, and waving an envelope.*

TINY. No show!

MARKETA. Not again.

TINY. He's cancelled it.
  And I have to read this out to you all…

SERENA (*gestures*). 'What is it? / Explain.'

TINY. It's a letter. What does it look like?

  TINY *turns and* SERENA *gives him the finger.* LILLIE *sees this and laughs.*

MARKETA. He'll be 'resting his voice' again. Hiding more like.

TINY. Now, you are to sit around and I'm to read this;
  slowly, deliberately and aloud.

MARKETA. Just tell us what it says.

TINY. I don't know, do I?
  All I know is he was up all night writing.
  And he wouldn't tell me anything about it.

GEORGE/GEORGINA. Up all night?

  Beat.

MARKETA. Well then.
  Read.
  Go on.

  TINY *opens the envelope and takes out a rather fat letter.*

TINY (*pompously*). 'My dear family,
  forgive me for passing on this great news…'

MARKETA. Great news?

TINY. Do you want to hear what the man has to say or not?

  While this exchange is going on, SERENA *has snatched the letter out of his hands and given it to* GEORGE/GEORGINA.

MARKETA. I'm not in the mood for slowly deliberately and aloud.

LILLIE. I agree.

TINY (*to* SERENA). You get above yourself, Miss.

SERENA (*gestures to* GEORGE/GEORGINA). 'Read.'

(*Gestures to* TINY.) 'Zip it.'

(*Gestures to* GEORGE/GEORGINA.) 'You, read. Go.'

GEORGE/GEORGINA (*in a caller's voice*). 'Forgive… me…
  for passing on this great news in such an impersonal fashion
  but I have decided to become an elective mute for two hours
  each day for the sake of an overworked voice.'

  MARKETA *rolls her eyes and curses* RILEY *in some
  unknown language.*

  'Hear what I have to say, through Tiny who is most kind…'

TINY. Through Tiny who has been usurped by a half-and-half…

MILLIE. You're doing great, keep going.

GEORGE/GEORGINA. 'The townies are staying away.
  Even in this new location we cannot draw a crowd.
  I know that I have hidden it well but for some time I have
  been gravely worried,
  and our enterprise has been in financial distress.'

MARKETA. Distress? Distress!
  He thinks we haven't noticed.

GEORGE/GEORGINA. 'I can no longer ignore the simple truth
  that tastes have changed.
  It seems that the only part of our repertoire that whets their
  appetite is the mermaid show,
  despite the obvious mechanism of its smoke-and-mirrors
  system.
  No offence to Miss Serena, of course, who performs it
  wonderfully and has been saving our bacon,
  so to speak.'

TINY. Bacon? Ha!

  SERENA *takes a mock-curtsy and then gestures for them to
  continue.*

GEORGE/GEORGINA. 'Understand it, I do not.
  Those of you who were once seen as God's marvels are now
  viewed as man's mistakes.

GEORGE/GEORGINA *scans the letter.*

Quite long.

LILLIE *and* MILLIE. Skip it.

SERENA *gestures impatiently.*

GEORGE/GEORGINA *skips the next five pages.*

TINY *mutters to himself in disapproval.*

GEORGE/GEORGINA. 'But fear not, family.
An idea has arrived.
I have been inspired by a man I met many years ago who was both a giant and a dwarf in his lifetime.
At age twenty-one he stood just three feet ten and one half inches tall.
By the time of his death he was seven feet eleven.'

MARKETA. I remember him.
Nice man.
Very ugly.

GEORGE/GEORGINA. 'Like him, what we will provide is an alternative view of the world.
A spectacle of hope.
A defiance of science.
Something that demonstrates the ability of the human spirit to overcome seemingly insurmountable obstacles.'

LILLIE. Isn't that the point as things are?

MARKETA. I can speak five languages.

TINY. Ha!

SERENA *claps her hands with impatience.*

GEORGE/GEORGINA. 'Something authentic, something more than real.
It's simple, my wonders. You have to...'

MARKETA. Yes?

GEORGE/GEORGINA. 'Change.'

TINY. What?

GEORGE/GEORGINA. 'Change. Alter. Adjust.
Show not only what makes you different but how much you want to be the same.
Be just like them, despite it all.
One of them, only more so.
In doing so you will fascinate.
In short, you must transform.'

SERENA *makes physical her displeasure for the ideas in the letter.*

Four

RILEY*'s private quarters.*

RILEY *is holding a watch in one hand and the other hand is raised as if about to start a race. Silence for a time. Occasionally* TINY *makes as if to speak and then stops himself. Then* RILEY *makes the signal that time is up and they launch into it:*

TINY. There's got to be another way.

RILEY. There isn't.

Beat.

We'll start with you.

TINY. Me?

RILEY. To…
To give the others courage.
Start with the main attraction.
Especially as we can be certain that *you* possess the requisite will-power.
You proved that when all this started.

TINY. That was a long time ago, Boss.

RILEY. Plumper friendlier times.

Dempsey's Sideshow.

You were standing beside me for such an age that I thought you worked there.

And then you said, out loud, like you were talking to yourself – What was it again?

TINY. 'I bet you could make a lot of money in a place like this.'

RILEY. Exactly that.

The bill was...

a pinhead, The Human Blister...

TINY. Jo-Jo the Dog-Faced Boy...

RILEY. And...

TINY. Happy Humphrey.

RILEY. The star.

TINY. He was so big there was nowhere else to look.

A face the size of a dinner plate.

RILEY. His little mouth almost lost within; tiny pearly whites peeking out.

I remember thinking it would be impossible for those teeth to chew all the food required.

TINY. It seemed like he was growing fatter off our stares even as we stood there.

Beat.

I multiplied the amount of money I paid to get in by the amount of patrons I counted.

RILEY. And you deduced that it wasn't the looking he was living off but the charge for the privilege.

TINY. When you said that you were to inherit a similar outfit it seemed like fate.

'Just give them genuine wonders and nothing else.'

No cons.

No blow-offs.

No gaffs.
No novelty acts.
Just marvels.
'Robert Riley's Odditorium.'
I was gripped.

RILEY. And when you said that you wanted to work for me.
I thought you meant on the crew!

TINY. I had discipline.
I had stamina.
Once I set my mind to something…

RILEY. Exactly.

Beat.

When you came back I didn't know you.
This colossus.
Just sitting there eating three steak dinners and waiting for me.
While a commotion of gaping raged all around.
And you said,
now let me get this right…

TINY. 'I just ate and ate and got fatter and fatter.'

RILEY. Well, my friend, it's time to repeat history.
Only in reverse.
Let's face it, you've already made a start.

Beat.

TINY. I think it's fair to say that gaining is easier than losing,
Boss.

RILEY. Nonsense.

TINY. But even if I did manage to do it, why would anyone
want to gape then?
I'd be… *run-of-the-mill*.

RILEY. Why?
Imagine this:
Ladies and gentlemen!

Boys and girls!
There stands before you now,
a man who is,
quite literally,
half the man he used to be.
A credit to human powers of will and determination.
Someone who has transformed himself from a sideshow fat-man
– flabby and ungainly
taking up far more than his fair share of space and air –
now renovated
through sheer power of grit, hard work and self-sacrifice into
a person you can be proud to look at...
a person just like you...
Et cetera. Et cetera.
It needs work obviously.
But they'll lap it up.
Don't you see?

TINY. I do.
And I'm not sure I like it.

RILEY. Let me reassure you, my friend.
You are never again going to be the man that I met at that show.
That man who was looking for his purpose in life.
No matter how much you lose.
He's not who we're selling.
The merchandise is two other Tinys.
The one that is now.
And the one that will be.
Don't you see?
That's the hook.
That's the thing townies will want to see.
The difference.

Five

GEORGE/GEORGINA *is preparing chopped lettuce, observed
by* LILLIE *and* MILLIE. *The sound of* SERENA*'s act and*
RILEY *calling it in the near distance. Ticket stubs and other
detritus on the ground.*

MILLIE. You could at least give him a tomato.

GEORGE/GEORGINA. Have my orders.
　　Boss made them very clear.

MILLIE. Poor Tiny.

LILLIE. I think it's funny.

　　MILLIE *looks at her.*

　　Well, we've all starved for his sake.

MILLIE. Not for his sake – for all our sakes.

　　Beat.

　　He dislikes onions.
　　G, did you hear me?

GEORGE/GEORGINA. Yes, Millie, dear.
　　Nothing but lettuce here.

　　Beat.

　　Plenty other things to do, you know.

MILLIE. Sorry.
　　It's not your fault.

　　GEORGE/GEORGINA *exits.*

LILLIE. I wish you could relax.
　　For once we don't have any chores.
　　No act to perform.
　　And you can't even take it easy.

MILLIE. We've got nothing to do.

LILLIE. Exactly.

MILLIE. You don't get it, do you?
    We've lost our place, Lil.
    Why feed us?
    Why keep us?

Beat.

LILLIE. And who's fault is that?
    I wasn't the one putting butter on Tiny's bread.
    I wasn't the one giving him bread to begin with.

MILLIE. He looked pale.
    I couldn't help it.

A smaller TINY *enters and takes a seat at his table, followed by* GEORGE/GEORGINA, *who presents his meal.* TINY *chews with feigned enthusiasm occasionally making 'mmm' noises. They all watch him for a time; like a freak show within the freak show.*

When he's finished, he gets up, stretches and begins jogging/exercising.

MARKETA *enters and watches too.*

MARKETA. I want to look away, but I can't.

GEORGE/GEORGINA. He's a man possessed.

TINY jogs by behind them, gives them a forced jaunty wave.

MARKETA. The incredible shrinking man.
    I have to admit,
    I didn't think he had it in him.
    So, ladies and… lady-gent,
    Serena's the only one on show.
    Riley refuses to talk about anything but this new way.
    And Tiny seems to have found a will of iron.
    Where does that leave us?

MILLIE. Stuck.

LILLIE. Not necessarily.

MILLIE. What are you going to do, Lillie?
    Go solo as a sleeping beauty?

LILLIE. No.
But we could make a gesture.
Something small,
just to keep Riley happy.

MARKETA. I don't think I can keep going like this,
doing nothing while Tiny's disappearing in front of me.
I'll go mad.

MILLIE. Not you as well!

MARKETA. Much as I hate to admit it,
there *is* something strangely appealing about watching Tiny
shrivel.

Beat.

I'd hate to become a relic.

MILLIE. What do you think, G?
You're very quiet.

GEORGE/GEORGINA. If there was something that could be
done,
would do it.
If Boss asked.
But what 'gesture' can George/Georgina make?

MARKETA. Different for you.
You're Riley's right hand.
Not going to cut you off,
so to speak,
is he?

After a moment…

GEORGE/GEORGINA. Don't know how it's going to be done.
But think we owe it to him to try and do it.
Do know one thing:
if Boss thinks there's a way to keep us together then better to
believe him than fight him.
Cos there's almost nothing in the safe.
And townies don't want us any more.
Least, not as we are.

Six

MARKETA *is alone*. SERENA *joins her.*

MARKETA. Thank you for coming.

> SERENA *nods.*

SERENA (*gestures*). 'What?'

> MARKETA *nods towards a cloth and* SERENA *picks it up*
> *to reveal a razor, shaving foam, etc. It takes a moment for the*
> *penny to drop.*

MARKETA. You're the only one I can trust not to make a fuss.

SERENA (*gestures*). 'No.'

MARKETA. Is it my body, or no?

> SERENA *looks at her.*

> Once I've made up my mind, that's it.
> So you can put those eyes away.

> SERENA *touches* MARKETA*'s beard.*

> The only part of my father that I got.
> My pride and show.

> *Beat.*

> Let's get it over with.

> SERENA *hesitates.*

> (*Indicating using a foot.*) Look, either you do it or I do it
> myself.

> SERENA *reluctantly gestures for* MARKETA *to sit down,*
> *takes out a shaving brush, razor and soap, and begins*
> *lathering* MARKETA*'s face.*

> Must be frustrating.

> SERENA *nods.*

> You have always been mute?

SERENA *shakes her head and continues to lather.*

And your feet as well?
A childhood illness or –

SERENA *shakes her head. She stops what she's doing. She tries to express seeing our world for the first time.*

No, I don't get it.
Simpler.

SERENA *tries again to express – 'obsession, looking' – which* MARKETA, *being* MARKETA, *reads as love.*

Love.

SERENA *makes a gesture, indicating 'sort of'. She tries to communicate another idea – 'naivety'.*

Stupid?

Again, SERENA*'s response is 'sort of'. It's a bit more complicated than that.*

Ah, don't worry.

I'm prying.
I'm usually much better at it.

SERENA (*gestures*). 'You talk.'

MARKETA. Alright.

What should I…?

SERENA *thinks for a moment. She makes a gesture that evokes* RILEY.

Riley?

SERENA *nods.*

Why him?

SERENA *shrugs.*

It's a long story.

SERENA (*gestures*). 'Continue.'

MARKETA. A sad story.

SERENA (*gestures*). 'Continue.'

MARKETA. With secrets…

> SERENA *makes a 'cross my heart' gesture with the razor.*
> SERENA *holds the razor near* MARKETA*'s throat.*
> MARKETA *nods.* SERENA *begins to shave her.*

When I was a very young woman a child was born to me.
A daughter.
I had been on the road for only one year.
I met a man.
A strongman.
I thought my baby would come out strong…
She was hairy, like me.
And she had arms.
Strongman's arms.
…She died.
She never breathed at all.
The people, the people I worked for, wanted for me to put
her in a jar,
pickled,
and let the townies peep.
I said no.
I asked a priest to bury her.
To baptise her.
He refused.
I went to the churchyard at night.
I said to the strongman 'Dig me a grave that is all I will ever
ask of you.'
He put her in the ground.

I travelled further.
I went to the city.
And I met Riley.
Before they dressed me as a wild woman and made me speak
gibberish.
Called me the missing link.
The knot that ties humans to apes.
But Riley gave me good clothes to wear and called me
Countess.

He said that a blue blood with hair on her face would mean
more.
And we could charge twice the price as I was twice
blessed.
Blessed, he said.
For years we made money together.

Silence.

I don't understand what you are doing here.
Don't you know we're dying?

SERENA *shakes her head vehemently. Perhaps there is a
painful attempt to make a sound.*

Stop, stop.

MARKETA *looks at her half-shaved face.*

Can you carry on?

SERENA *picks up the razor and begins again.*

Sometimes there are men who want to see me alone.
They slip a note or give a nod or buy a present.
Sometimes I do that.
It's not...
I never...
Mainly they just want a closer look.
At the shows they can see only one thing or the other.
They see I have no arms, they see I have a beard, they see
I have no arms and back again.
But alone, with less clothes, they can take in the whole
and they glaze over like the fish you caught.
In their heads they bring along wives, or women they have
seen in magazines or dreams.
But after they leave, when they close their eyes, they can see
only me.
They pay for the privilege.
A few towns back one wanted to give me more.
Said I could go with him.
Settle down.
I thought I should: that I could no longer stand the struggle.

SERENA (*gestures*). 'So? Why didn't you?'

MARKETA. It's not that simple.
A long time ago Riley had a wife.
He had a mother too.
Mother was a legless wonder.
Wife a tattooed lady.
They didn't get along.
Jealousies.
The billing.
His mother got a better offer somewhere else.
His wife ran off with a lion tamer.
And Riley got smaller.

Beat.

I couldn't stand to see it.
In the end, the show is all he has.
It's how *we* look after *him*.

SERENA *shows* MARKETA *herself in the mirror. Her beard is gone.*

I look old.

Beat.

I can always grow it back.

SERENA *picks up some of the hair and tries it on her own face.*

Seven

LILLIE, MILLIE *and* GEORGE/GEORGINA *sit together.*
LILLIE *and* MILLIE *are still dressed identically, but in different colours. Litter and evidence of increasing audience sizes scattered around. The sound of* TINY*'s act in the distance and* RILEY *calling it.*

MILLIE *is trying to read but is distracted by the sound of* TINY*'s act.*

GEORGE/GEORGINA *is scrubbing clothes in a bucket of water.*

SERENA *enters, sits by* LILLIE. LILLIE *applies* SERENA*'s make-up and helps with her hair. An intimacy between them.*

A loud cheer from the show can be heard. MILLIE *winces.*

MILLIE. All I'm saying is that it's not fair.

GEORGE/GEORGINA. Ah,
    not finished this yet.

Beat.

Trust Mr Riley, yes?

MILLIE. Yes.
    Of course.

GEORGE/GEORGINA. Well then.
    Trust that he knows what he's doing.

MILLIE. As far as I can see, *he's* not doing anything.

GEORGE/GEORGINA. Millie!

MILLIE. Sorry.

Beat.

I can't see it.
That's all.
Tiny is one thing.
But the rest of us aren't made.
We're reals.
Never known anything else.
And we can't exactly be unrealed, can we?
Trusting Mr Riley isn't going to change that.

GEORGE/GEORGINA. The point is you have to try.
    The show will be worked out.
    In time.

Millie doesn't need to see it.
George/Georgina doesn't even need to see it.
Boss sees it.

Beat.

Rather go back to the way things were?
To the no hope?

MILLIE. No.

GEORGE/GEORGINA. Well then.

MILLIE. *Do* you see it?

Beat.

GEORGE/GEORGINA. No.
Not completely.
But that doesn't matter.
'It's not the act, it's the…'

MILLIE (*interrupting*). Yeah, yeah, yeah.

Beat.

Lillie and me are bottom of the pile now.
Just because we're more complicated than others.

GEORGE/GEORGINA. Not bottom of the pile.
Don't be silly.
And not more complicated than all.

MILLIE. Well, that's a matter of debate.

GEORGE/GEORGINA. Is it?

LILLIE. Shh!
Do you mind?
I'm trying to concentrate.

MILLIE. Sorry for living.

LILLIE. Give it a rest.

SERENA (*gestures*). 'Stop. Let her alone.'

LILLIE. Okay then.
   Bye.

LILLIE turns away.

MILLIE *casts a look at* GEORGE/GEORGINA *and then goes back to her book.*

LILLIE *whispers in* SERENA*'s ear.* SERENA *smiles.* LILLIE *whispers in* SERENA*'s ear.* SERENA *makes a gesture.* LILLIE *doesn't understand so* SERENA *starts to scratch something on the ground.* MILLIE *notices and is irritated by all this.* GEORGE/GEORGINA *concentrates on the washing in the bucket.* LILLIE *shakes her head.*

(*Signs.*) I can't read.
   We had an owner.
   He bought us from our mother.
   He tried to teach us.

For me, the words danced.
   I was bored.
   So,
   I darned.
   Millie learned.

SERENA (*gestures*). 'Sad.'

LILLIE (*signs*). But Mr Riley found us.
   And then it wasn't so bad.

Beat.

There is a moment of stillness. LILLIE *and* SERENA *close,* MILLIE *worried,* GEORGE/GEORGINA *seeing all. It's broken when* LILLIE *whispers in* SERENA*'s ear again.*

MILLIE. Stop it!

She imitates whispering

That noise.

SERENA *is confused.*

LILLIE (*aloud*). She's afraid I like you better.
It makes us shiver.

SERENA *pulls away from* LILLIE, *who sulks at this. She looks to* GEORGE/GEORGINA, *who is no help. She tries to catch* MILLIE's *eye but* MILLIE *will not look at her.*

RILEY *enters with* TINY, *who is now actually tiny.*

RILEY. Amazing, my friend.
Amazing.
My favourite was the puddingy woman who asked for the secrets to your success.
Extraordinary.
You were heroic.
Actually heroic.
I've never seen anything like it.

MILLIE (*mocking*). 'I've never seen anything like it.' Ha!

RILEY. Excuse me?

MILLIE. Nothing.

RILEY. Yes.
Well, I don't know what you are all looking so glum for.
Everyone is getting paid this month.

MILLIE. Really?

RILEY. Proportionately.
Of course.

Beat.

Considering the difference in effort being exerted, I think that's only fair.

GEORGE/GEORGINA. What about the code?

RILEY. I'm sorry?
George/Georgina, you have a question?

GEORGE/GEORGINA. Equal wages.
All paid the same whether top of the billing or bottom.
Your idea.

RILEY. But these are unusual circumstances, are they not?

GEORGE/GEORGINA. Yes,
   but…

RILEY. Unless, of course, you'd rather we went back to no
   wages at all?

   SERENA *writes something and hands* RILEY *a piece of
   paper, but he doesn't read it.*

   No time.
   Your public awaits.
   Well –
   I think it's safe to say they're Tiny's public now.

   RILEY *obliviously picks up a seething* SERENA *and carries
   her off to the show.*

   TINY *and* GEORGE/GEORGINA *exit in opposite
   directions.* MILLIE *places her head on* LILLIE'*s shoulder
   and* LILLIE *strokes her hair.*

LILLIE. We're getting paid.

MILLIE. Proportionately.

LILLIE. Yes, but still.
   You need new books.
   And we could get some ribbon maybe.

MILLIE. That'd be nice.

   MARKETA *enters. Her beard has been shaved off and she's
   wearing a cloak or other clothes that disguise her lack of
   arms. She's dressed differently too – in a more overtly
   feminine way.*

MARKETA. Well, girls.

   What do you think?

   MILLIE *covers her eyes.*

LILLIE. It's beautiful.
   You're beautiful.

Eight

RILEY *and* SERENA *in* RILEY*'s quarters, after* SERENA*'s act.* SERENA *is drying herself with a towel.*

RILEY. And so what I'm proposing is a gradual fading out of
the mermaid act over the next few days, alongside the public
unveiling of the new Countess and, well… something big
I've got planned for later.

I'm going to increase the number of shows Tiny is doing and
play up the suspense of what might be about to happen
between the two of them…

Beat.

It's a surprise.

Beat.

A marvellous surprise.

Beat.

Alright, you wore me down; it's a wedding.

SERENA *just looks at him.*

My fear is that your act lacks the sincerity now demanded by
our new 'style'.
But of course we wouldn't want to lose you.
I'm not the kind of man to disregard all that you've done
for us.

SERENA (*gestures*). 'Yes, so?'

RILEY. Well,
and this is somewhat delicate,
the Countess is eventually going to need arms, hands of
some sort and I'm looking into it…

But in the meantime I wondered if you wouldn't mind
filling in.
Helping her with day-to-day tasks;

the shaving, seeing as you've already done such a good job there,
and whatever else needs doing.

SERENA *shakes her head and steps back.*

All very well looking like a feminine beardless creature,
but she's going to have to start wearing shoes.
Feet, apparently, are unseemly.
And that's where you come in.

SERENA (*gestures*). 'No.'

RILEY. Of course, you have options…
If you choose to cut your losses, no harm done and warm wishes.

SERENA *just looks at him.*

If you don't mind me saying so, talking to you is a bit like dropping pennies in a well.
I'm not sure you realise that these are adults, with their own minds.
Who make their own decisions.
They voice their thoughts.
And they understand
That if you live as we live
You must put family first.
Perhaps if you'd been with us a little longer…
But there isn't time to school you now.

SERENA *writes something and offers it to him but he ignores it. He won't look at her now.*

Sometimes they have to be coaxed, yes.
Persauded.
We don't always know what's best for us.
And a parent must teach a child to eat their greens.
Sometimes by whatever means necessary.

SERENA *writes something and offers it to him but he ignores it.*

Look here.
I have ground my teeth, pulled out my hair in handfuls,
paced floors and had many sleepless nights.
But I have done my duty and found a solution.
And it works.
We are started once more.
The relief.
The relief!
Well, you simply can't.
I doubt it anyway.
That you can come close to imagining the relief.
Can you?
Can you?

SERENA *shakes her head. She breaks something to get him to look at her.*

SERENA (*gestures*). 'Oops.'

As they bend down to pick up the pieces:

RILEY. I'm just trying to preserve a way of life.

SERENA *looks around. She can't find any paper. She picks up a pen or paint or chalk. She looks around and then she writes upon the wall or tent canvas.*

She writes: 'THINK AGAIN.'

RILEY *tries to stop her and attempts to take the pen from her. But she is surprisingly strong. There is a stand-off: a moment of being opposite but equal forces between them.*

GEORGE/GEORGINA *is heading to* RILEY's *quarters and observes some of this through a window/or an opening, without being seen. When it gets too much* GEORGE/ GEORGINA *makes a noise. The spell is broken.* SERENA *leaves.*

As she leaves, RILEY *says loudly, and to no one in particular:*

Nowhere else to go?
Well well, there there.
Always welcome here.
You can start your new duties as soon as you like.

*There is a knock, or a cough. He straightens himself and
returns to his desk.*

What?!
I'm busy.

Peeping gingerly around, GEORGE/GEORGINA *is taken
aback by the writing on the wall, but tries to ignore it.*

GEORGE/GEORGINA. Takings, Boss.

RILEY. Fine.
I'm just…
I had a word with Miss Serena about her duties.

GEORGE/GEORGINA. Yes.
Was hearing.

RILEY. Were you?

GEORGE/GEORGINA. Not listening but…
But was counting and could hear.

RILEY. What's the count?

GEORGE/GEORGINA. Up another twenty per cent.
Selling more of Tiny's old postcards each show than in a
week of befores.
Yesterday the queue went all the way round the wagon.
Could easily move indoors now.

RILEY. No, not yet.
We have to be patient.
There is still much more to be done.
The trick is to perfect everyone here where it doesn't matter
so much,
and then roll into the city with something watertight.

Beat. GEORGE/GEORGINA *is unclear about whether to
stay or go.*

RILEY. One more thing.

GEORGE/GEORGINA. Something you need?

RILEY. You never really grew to like it, did you?
  The looking.

GEORGE/GEORGINA. Not the looking, no.

RILEY. You're finding this difficult?
  This new approach?

GEORGE/GEORGINA *nods*.

  Still, I was thinking.
  Perhaps, if you were to become one or the other?
  If you were to choose.
  Perhaps there's a way to sell that?

GEORGE/GEORGINA. Can sweep the floors, can light the fires,
  can boil the water, can gather the wood, can mend the wagon,
  can wash the clothes, can count the money, can hammer the
  pegs, but can't ever just choose to be one or the other.
  You know that too.
  You've not looked at George/Georgina in days.
  You know they would never clap hands for that.
  Not while underneath the bothness is there.

RILEY. No, I don't think they would, would they?
  However, there may be another option.
  A doctor.
  He's coming to look at the twins.

GEORGE/GEORGINA. A doctor?

RILEY. A surgeon, actually.

GEORGE/GEORGINA. A surgeon.
  For… halving?

RILEY. He says there's a way to do it.
  Leaving each with only a minor impairment.
  Of course, it won't be cheap.
  But the sooner we do it, the sooner we can recoup the cost.
  It's vital that we are restored to our full complement before
  the summer festivals.

  Pause.

Do you think it's wrong of me?
A way forward for them, I thought, but maybe you think otherwise.

GEORGE/GEORGINA. No.
They've been worried.
Arguing.
Asking questions.

Beat.

Is it dangerous?

RILEY. I'll be guided by him.
About your situation also.
I'll ask.
He may be able to help.

GEORGE/GEORGINA. Me as a girl, a girl alone.

RILEY (*returning to his paperwork*). Well,
or a boy,
depending...
Anyway, lots to do...

Pause.

RILEY *returns to his papers but* GEORGE/GEORGINA *doesn't move.*

GEORGE/GEORGINA. Have a question.

RILEY. Quickly.

GEORGE/GEORGINA. Shows have always been simple.
Oddities right there in front of them.
Immediate, undeniable.
Right?

RILEY. You're teaching your granny to suck eggs.

GEORGE/GEORGINA. Indeed.
Of course.
But, with these new *versions* of us.
Well, won't they lose their power, over time?

The further away we get from what we were.
Mean, will anyone come back for a second look?

Beat.

RILEY. You're failing to grasp the fundamentals.
Looking is only the start.
It's about telling a story, like I've always said,
only more so.
How two bodies can belong to one person and what
happened on the journey in between.
The thing that captures them
isn't what they *see* at all.
It's their own potential.

GEORGE/GEORGINA. But –

RILEY. You don't think there's a merit in inspiring people?
You, who have always understood this game,
you don't see how much we stand to gain by turning the
glass away from ourselves and on to the lookers?

Beat.

That's disappointing.

GEORGE/GEORGINA *doesn't respond.*

Alright.
It's time for my silence.
That's all then?

GEORGE/GEORGINA. That's all.

GEORGE/GEORGINA *is about to leave.*

RILEY Oh, do me a favour.
Get rid of that.

RILEY *gestures to the wall without looking at it. In the
transition,* GEORGE/GEORGINA *fetches a bucket and
starts to scrub.*

Nine

LILLIE *and* MILLIE *are sewing a wedding dress for*
MARKETA, *their four hands dancing.*

LILLIE *has dyed her hair and they are no longer dressed
identically.*

MILLIE. You're crooked, Lil.

LILLIE. Am I?

MILLIE. You are.
  Your head's elsewhere.
  Look.

LILLIE. It's not.
  But I'm happy to rip the stitches.
  If you would like.

MILLIE. Why not just sew straight in the first place?

  Beat.

LILLIE. It's exciting, Mil.
  Don't you think?
  I think it's exciting.

MILLIE. Imagine marrying *him*, though…

  They laugh.

LILLIE. Ew!
  Imagine him in his underwear.

MILLIE (*laughing*). No!
  I don't want to.

LILLIE. Imagine him kissing.

MILLIE. Stop it, Lillie!

LILLIE. Imagine if you woke up one morning and he was lying
  there beside you all fat again and there was nothing you
  could do about it.

MILLIE. That won't happen, will it?
  He might roll over and smother her.

LILLIE. A terrible way to die.

  Beat.

  I suppose she's stuck with him now.
  No matter what.

MILLIE. I suppose so.
  But –
  at least they have a someone now.
  They won't be lonely.

  Beat.

  It might not be that bad.

LILLIE. She might regret it.

MILLIE. Nothing terrible will happen.
  Mr Riley wouldn't let it.
  Would he?

LILLIE. No, Mil.
  I don't think so.

  Beat.

  Still, we've never been to a wedding before.

MILLIE. That's true.
  There'll be crowds.
  I hope we'll be able to see.

LILLIE. A pity we can't be bridesmaids.
  I would like to stand beside her.
  And hold her bouquet.

MILLIE. It was only that Mr Riley thought...
  There wasn't time.
  Not to make us clothes as well.
  And it's been a rush and...

LILLIE (*interrupting*). It wasn't that, Mil.
　　He doesn't want…
　　The distraction.

　　Beat.

MILLIE. We've tried.
　　He can't say we haven't.
　　I don't know you now.
　　Your hair.

　　Beat.

　　Besides,
　　if it works,
　　G says that Mr Riley says,
　　there's going to be a wedding in every town.
　　Bigger and better each go round.
　　So we could get a chance some other time.

LILLIE. Could be sooner rather than later…

　　Pause.

　　What did you think of his friend?
　　The doctor.

MILLIE. I told you I don't want to talk about it.

LILLIE. I'm not talking about *it*.
　　I'm only asking what you thought of the doctor himself.

MILLIE. In what way?

LILLIE. As a man, Mil.

MILLIE. He seemed nice,
　　I suppose.
　　Full of his own importance.

LILLIE. I thought he was handsome.

MILLIE. I know you did.
　　It was obvious.

LILLIE. What do you mean?

MILLIE. I perceived a certain weakness of the knees.
Felt a heart flutter.
Your eyes like saucers.
Just like in books.

LILLIE. I wouldn't know, would I?

Beat.

It wasn't him that did that.

MILLIE. Was it not?

LILLIE. It was what he was saying.
I got such a fright.

MILLIE. I told you.
I won't…

LILLIE. You won't even consider it?

MILLIE. No.
I…
Maybe.
I…
I can't.

LILLIE. Not even for Mr Riley's sake?
After everything he's done.
Things could be worse, Mil.
Don't forget.
And we wouldn't be bottom of the heap any more.
We'd trump a silly old wedding any time.

MILLIE. I know but…
It's not about that.

LILLIE. You're right.
It's scary.

MILLIE. It's not scary, Lil.
It's not scary.
The dark is scary.
Ghosts are scary.
It's more.
It's much more than that.

LILLIE. It will probably all come to nothing anyway.
    It's alright.

Beat.

But he won't know if we don't let him look.

Beat.

It's not that you are a weight around my neck, Mil.
    I know you think I think that.
    It's that I've been dragging you down.

MILLIE (*puts her fingers in her ears*). I'm not listening!
    Stop it, Lillie!
    Please.
    Leave me be

LILLIE *stops.*

Pause.

LILLIE. Just let him look, Mil.
    That's all.

MILLIE. I don't know you.
    Your hair.

Beat.

LILLIE. Please.

MILLIE. And if he looks, then what?

LILLIE. We'll see.

Pause.

MILLIE. We'd have to take our clothes off.
    In front of him.

LILLIE. I know.

MILLIE. You'd like to.

LILLIE. A bit.

Ten

Night.

For an earlier performance, a table was laid with cream pies to demonstrate the new TINY*'s self-discipline. A sign at the table reads 'Witness His Amazing Self-Control!!!'*

The show is over and TINY *sneaks back to the pies.*

TINY *looks around to make sure he is alone.*

He takes a napkin from his pocket and delicately places it around his neck. Then ravenously, greedily, he eats one of the pies. He almost inhales it.

TINY *sits there, realising what he has done. He sobs and tries not to be heard.*

TINY *picks up one of the other pies and hits himself in the face with it.*

TINY *picks up another pie and hits himself in the face with it.*

TINY *picks up another pie and hits himself in the face with it.*

All the pies are gone.

TINY *wipes his face, uncovers the mirror, checks his reflection, practises his smile, re-covers the mirror and walks away.*

Eleven

Elsewhere SERENA *is lathering* MARKETA*'s face.*

MARKETA. Listen to this.
Ahem.
'Robert Riley's show is a piece of entertainment certainly and soon to dazzle city audiences but it is also more than that and makes me think: Perhaps even the most wanton amongst us have the power to change within.'

'How astounded was I to witness the powerful change in the
Countess Marketa.'
Poor Tiny,
He's hardly mentioned at all.

A stroke of the razor.

'As a long-time critic of the travelling raree show it felt
wrong to be inside the tents where once played out
exploitation…'
Blah. Blah. Blah.
'…but the transformation is astonishing and despite my
previous position I can now completely understand why the
public are in love with this extraordinary woman.'
Extraordinary.
Pretty damn good.

SERENA *weeps angry tears.*

A stroke of the razor.

'Now she is the most feminine of feminine creatures, her
beautiful and fine-featured face no longer hidden behind a
bristling beard any man would be proud of. And this only
serves to highlight the good breeding she has always
possessed.'

'Only her missing arms reassure you that it is the same
woman.'
Not for long, Mr Journalist.
Just you wait.
I got a letter today.
From a man,
An engineer.

Beat.

He wants to make me arms.

A stroke of the razor.

He sent me some drawings.
Maybe townies are better than I think they are?
Do you think that?

SERENA (*gestures*). 'No.'

She wipes the shaving foam vigorously from MARKETA*'s face.*

SERENA *wipes her eyes.*

She hesitates for a moment and then makes a sound. A small one. It seems to cause her pain. She tries again, and she becomes unsteady on her feet. The pain is worse.

MARKETA. Are you alright?

SERENA *steadies herself.*

I don't know what you're getting so worked up about.
There's still a future in all this.
We're not dying any more.

SERENA *exits.*

Twelve

After a show…

More show detritus scattered about.

Everyone is present.

TINY *is wearing his new smile, apparently delighted with the crowd's response.*

GEORGE/GEORGINA *is standing beside* RILEY, *taking his jacket and hat as he discards them. Similarly a glum* SERENA *takes various items of* MARKETA*'s clothing.*

MILLIE *and* LILLIE *are sitting, by the stove, looking up.*

RILEY. That went wonderfully but there's work to be done.
We've introduced them to the denuded Marketa.
We've told them that she's Tiny's bride-to-be.
We've ordered the 'happy couple' publicity postcards.

So, you can imagine my shock when I learned yesterday that the groom doesn't know how to waltz.

TINY *looks contrite*.

TINY. I never had much call for dancing before, Boss.

RILEY. Everything must be perfect.
And so: a lesson.

MILLIE. For everyone?

LILLIE (*pointedly to* RILEY). I'd like that.

RILEY. Why not?
Except Miss Serena, of course.
Who I've asked to man the gramophone.

SERENA *takes up her position beside the gramophone*.
RILEY *opens a book*.

TINY *and* MARKETA *stand beside each other and*
GEORGE/GEORGINA *stands next to* LILLIE *and* MILLIE.

Now, Tiny, you're in charge.

And I suppose George/Georgina can be the, eh... leader in this... trio.
I'll cut in once we're established.
Now.
'Get into position by facing your partner.'
Or partners.
Ha ha.
'If you are the man – so to speak – place your right hand on your partner's waist slightly around the back.'
Okay, that looks right.
'And then extend your left hand to your side with your elbow bent and your palm raised facing her.
With that hand, grasp your partner's right hand in a loose grip and make sure your partner has...'

TINY. Boss?

RILEY. Ah, yes.
Apologies.

It would seem a slight adaptation is in order.
Perhaps just put your left hand on her shoulder instead.

TINY. Like this?

RILEY. That'll do.
And you, George/Georgina:
How about your hand on Millie's waist... yes?
And the other in Lillie's hand.
Excellent.

Step two.

'On the first beat, step forward gracefully with your left foot.
Your partner should follow your lead by doing the opposite
of what you do on each beat – in this case, stepping back
with her right foot.'
Got it?

TINY. Ouch.

MARKETA. Sorry, it's the shoes.
I can't get used to them.

MARKETA *winks at* SERENA, *who smiles a half-smile back.*

GEORGE/GEORGINA. Em... not sure, Boss.
Is this right?

RILEY. Great.

Step three.

'On the second beat, step forward and to the right with your
right foot. Trace an upside-down letter L in the air with your
foot as you do this.'

TINY. A what?

LILLIE. What do letters have to do with dancing?

MARKETA. Is this going to take all night?
I already know how to dance.

RILEY. Step four.

'Shift your weight to your right foot. Keep your left foot
stationary.'

Well… shift your weight to your right foot and keep your left foot stationary.

Are you doing it or not?

MILLIE. It really isn't that hard if you just count 'one two three, one two three'.
It's only waltzing.

MILLIE and LILLIE let go of GEORGE/GEORGINA and begin demonstrating with each other.
GEORGE/GEORGINA, still twirling and silently counting, approaches RILEY without thinking; placing a hand on RILEY's shoulder. RILEY looks up from his book.

GEORGE/GEORGINA meets RILEY's eye, takes a step away and blushes. RILEY is momentarily discombobulated.

RILEY. It would appear my book is a dud.

The others look on as MILLIE and LILLIE dance their slightly awkward waltz, with MILLIE counting…

Then MARKETA and TINY join in.

TINY. One two three.
One two three.
Do you enjoy it?
One two three.

MARKETA. What?

TINY. Being back up there?

MARKETA. Course.
Only reason I agreed to all this.

TINY. One two three.
Oh?

MARKETA. I don't know how to be myself without eyes on me.
Bit of a relief to know it still feels more or less the same.

TINY. But it's better, surely?

MARKETA. Looks are looks to me.
And money is money to Riley.

TINY. No, I think there's a difference.
I think we're doing more than entertaining.
I think we're educating too.

MARKETA. About what?

TINY. Hope.

MARKETA. Ha! About economics.
And novelties.

Beat.

Well?
Aren't you and I the biggest novelty act of them all?

TINY. You're a very cynical fiancée.

MARKETA. You!
Better to think of me as your leading lady, don't you think?
Like an actor.
So there's no confusion.
Now, are you in charge, or am I?

TINY steps on MARKETA's foot.

Ouch!

TINY. Sorry.

By now the other four have formed an awkward quartet:
LILLIE dancing with RILEY and MILLIE with
GEORGE/GEORGINA. MILLIE is teaching
GEORGE/GEORGINA, counting and encouraging. At
opportune moments LILLIE whispers covertly into RILEY's
ear and RILEY whispers back, the conversation growing
more bold as time goes on. SERENA follows LILLIE and
RILEY with her eyes.

The record putters to a halt. Everyone stops dancing and
looks towards SERENA.

RILEY. You have to wind it.

SERENA shrugs.

Wind the handle.
Are you simple after all?
The handle!
Must I do everything myself?

While RILEY *is winding the gramophone,* SERENA *stares at* LILLIE. *Everyone follows her gaze.*

LILLIE. What?

SERENA (*gestures*). 'WHISPERING.'

LILLIE. Sorry, I don't understand.

MILLIE. Whispering, she means whispering.

Beat.

What have you been whispering, Lil?

LILLIE. Mind your own business, Mil.

SERENA *makes the gesture bigger and bigger and brings it closer and closer to* LILLIE. *It's confrontational.*

GEORGE/GEORGINA. Miss Serena: think you should stop.

GEORGE/GEORGINA *restrains* SERENA.

LILLIE. No, sorry.
I'm afraid I don't get you.
You're not like us, not one of us.
You're just a townie, who can't talk.

SERENA *doesn't know what to sign back. She drops her hands.*

The gramophone putters back into action. RILEY *walks past her back to the group. They ignore her and begin a faltering dance practice once more.* RILEY *encourages them to keep dancing, around* SERENA. SERENA *opens her mouth, nothing comes out. Then she opens it again and tries to make a sound. It's difficult. Then she opens it again and makes a low, loud, guttural otherworldly noise. As she does so, her legs give out and she drops to the floor.*

Thirteen

GEORGE/GEORGINA *pushes* SERENA *in a wheelbarrow.*
RILEY *walks alongside carrying a bucket of water.* SERENA *is
unconscious. Also in the barrow are* SERENA'*s tail and a
suitcase.*

GEORGE/GEORGINA *stops and tries to rouse* SERENA *by
shaking her. It doesn't work so* RILEY *gives*
GEORGE/GEORGINA *the bucket, pointedly.*
GEORGE/GEORGINA *steps away and throws the water from
the bucket over* SERENA. SERENA *wakes with a start.*

GEORGE/GEORGINA. Thought
 Thought you might be dead.
 Couldn't see your chest move.

> SERENA *puts her hands to her throat. It's sore. Again*
> RILEY *gives the nod to* GEORGE/GEORGINA –

 Mr Riley
 We…
 Don't want you anymore.
 Here's some money. And a map.
 Will take you wherever you like within three miles.

Beat.

 Thank you for your time.

> SERENA *holds* GEORGE/GEORGINA'*s gaze until*
> GEORGE/GEORGINA *looks away. She doesn't accept the
> money or map.*

 Father sometimes went to sea.
 Used to say a mermaid foretells disaster.
 Keep thinking 'bout that.

RILEY. There isn't time for chit chat.
 I've got a show to call.

Beat.

Don't think of coming back, or causing trouble.
I can see now you are a poisonous person.
Full of foolish beliefs.
I should never have let you influence the others.
Never entertained a novelty.

SERENA *just looks at him.*

Looking at me like that.
Trying to bore a hole in me with those eyes.
To make me feel what?
Guilty?
What should I have done?
Walked away and left them to their own devices.

SERENA *makes a sound.*

Who are you to criticise me?
A novelty.
A loner.
I see now, you are quite unhinged.

SERENA *begins to speak. An otherworldly element to her
voice. She can also incorporate the gestural language she
has used previously in the play if that feels right.*

SERENA. L... L... Listen.
    Listen can't you for a change.
    You're always shouting.
    Always talking.
    Preaching wonder, but cannot see it any more.

RILEY. Ah-ha! Now we see it. Now we know.
    She's nothing but an old-fashioned fraud.

SERENA. Listen, listen.
    Your voice always in my head.
    Your voice woke me.
    Calling curiosities from the pier.
    Woke me from a place where everyone is perfect and
    everyone is the same.
    Heard. Heard a world. Saw. Saw a world. Seemed larger and
    more various than my own.

I went to the witch. She said I know what you want. There will be great pain. Every step shall feel as if you are treading on sharp knives.

I said I would bear it.

She said, I must be paid. You have the sweetest voice. This you must give to me.

And so I gave up my tongue for the chance of something different.

After hospitals and nuns were done with me.

I saw how this world really treats variation.

I read about your show and saw it bleed out of the paper.

I got older. Inside.

And then, one day, I found that voice again. The voice that spoke of marvels.

And you were all so much more beautiful than I had imagined. But so sad.

I thought, wearing a tail, I thought maybe I could help.

Hide in plain sight.

Bring in enough to eat at least.

But you. You: lost man with a big idea.

Making them strange to themselves.

While you cower behind.

Watching this creeping blandness

It appears that there is a limit to what I can endure.

RILEY. So that's your story?

Beat.

I've heard better.

She moves in a way that suggests the transformation that is happening within her. RILEY *is frightened and backs away.*

(*To* GEORGE/GEORGINA.) You can handle this from here?

GEORGE/GEORGINA *nods.*

He leaves, the wind knocked out of him, but the bravado still there. SERENA *looks after him.*

GEORGE/GEORGINA. Have the fish-knife in my pocket so… Just so you know.

SERENA. You're afraid of me?

GEORGE/GEORGINA. Don't know what you are.

SERENA. You sound like one of them.
  He's changing you already.

  Beat.

  Totally blinded to the beauty you possess
  Here
  Looking at me
  Right now.

  Beat.

GEORGE/GEORGINA. Where to?

SERENA. Back to the sea.

  A flash of gills. They leave.

Fourteen

MILLIE *and* LILLIE *lying on blankets on the ground.*

LILLIE *has fallen asleep.* MILLIE *is agitated but unable to move without waking her sister. If she could, she would get up and pace about.* GEORGE/GEORGINA *comes and sits beside them…*

MILLIE. Are you alright?

  Is she gone?

  Did she cry?

GEORGE/GEORGINA. Not to speak of it.

MILLIE. It's only me, G.

GEORGE/GEORGINA. Still, would rather not.

  Beat.

It was a lot for him to ask.
Frightening to be alone.

Beat.

And she. She...

MILLIE. I'm glad she's gone.
Don't worry, G.

Silence for a while.

MILLIE *looks at her sleeping sister.*

Lillie's dreaming...

GEORGE/GEORGINA *looks too.*

GEORGE/GEORGINA. Just a dream.
It doesn't mean anything.

MILLIE. When she dreams, she has a body of her own, she says.
I think that's why she always wants to sleep so much.

Beat.

Am I really that bad?

GEORGE/GEORGINA. She just is restless.
It's not your fault.

MILLIE. But it is.
Of course it is.

Beat.

Do *you* think we should do it?

GEORGE/GEORGINA. Well, it's there now, an option.
And if that's what Riley sees...

Beat.

But no,
think you should do what you want, Millie.
Isn't something you can do for him.
Never thought would say that.
But, he doesn't have to live with the results.

MILLIE. That's the thing, isn't it?

Lillie says 'yes, yes, yes'.

She's my sister and I don't want to deny her something that she wants so much.

But I've never been alone.

I've never been anywhere she hasn't been.

Never said anything she hasn't heard.

When she dies, I'll die.

To me that's a comfort.

Sometimes I think I'm a very old lady attached to a very young girl.

Beat.

Would you do it, G?

If there was an operation to change you...

GEORGE/GEORGINA. Doctor says there might be.

Wait and see.

He's pondering on it.

He measured with a ruler.

MILLIE. He used that on us as well.

Horrible feeling: metal up against our skin.

Did he draw big black lines on you?

GEORGE/GEORGINA. Took out his pen.

But didn't know where to start.

They laugh.

MILLIE. Will you?

GEORGE/GEORGINA. Can't decide.

Have been thinking today.

Remembering.

About Mother.

How when she was first pregnant she went to see a show.

Didn't tell Father.

There was a caller there.

And he said that the lobster-clawed woman was lobster-clawed because her mother had lobster cravings while she was expecting.

Talked about Merrick too.

Even Mother knew who that was.

And this caller said it was common knowledge that
Merrick's mother had been frightened by a circus elephant.

And that's why she gave birth to The Elephant Man.

Now Mother took this as a warning.

Never ate coal or pickles or anything else out of the ordinary.
No matter how much she craved.

Stayed in for fear of seeing something – anything – that
might make an impression.

Eventually she had to tell Father because he found her
weeping with fear.

Course, he said it was just a conman's trick and not to be so
foolish.

And when an ordinary little girl was born she was inclined to
agree.

It became the family joke.

But later, when she realised that her ordinary girl was
actually a little of both and neither of either, she was heard to
mutter

'I never could make up my mind whether I wanted a boy or a
girl.'

That's why George/Georgina joined the shows.

Not because the caller was telling Mother anything more
than a tale.

But because that caller captured her imagination more than
anything before or since.

Couldn't have own old life any more.

But could at least play a part in something as powerful as that.

And that's what Riley loves too.

(*The word 'me' is difficult to say but said deliberately.*) But
now, Millie, it feels like he is asking me to go back to being
the scared person who was stripped of clothes in a barn and
beaten by boys from the village.

Only he's asking me to stand beside and point at the same
time.

MILLIE *has fallen asleep.*

GEORGE/GEORGINA *covers her in a blanket and exits.*

When GEORGE/GEORGINA *has left,* LILLIE *sits up slightly.*

She looks down at her sleeping sister.

She touches her face.

MILLIE *begins to stir.*

LILLIE *pours something from a bottle onto a piece of cotton.
(Or she can can pull out a needle if that feels more
appropriate to the production.)*

MILLIE, *awake, turns her head.*

MILLIE (*dreamily*). Are we cold?

LILLIE *holds the cotton over her sister's mouth until*
MILLIE *passes out. (Or otherwise sedates her.)*

*Almost immediately she begins to feel the effects on herself
as well.*

LILLIE *cries out, sees* RILEY *approaching, then slumps.*

With great difficulty, he drags the sisters away.

*Something to indicate the passage of time, and something to
indicate the rupture. Perhaps the set breaking apart or being
dismantled. Sound. It's overwhelming.*

Fifteen

RILEY, MARKETA, TINY, LILLIE *and*
GEORGE/GEORGINA *stand where the camp once was.*

MARKETA, TINY, RILEY *and* LILLIE *are preparing to leave.*

They dismantle the camp.

They each have bags, apart from LILLIE *who sits in a
wheelchair, motionless.*

*By now the space is completely littered with the detritus of the
shows: ticket stubs, sweet wrappers, etc.*

GEORGE/GEORGINA *sits alone, head hanging*.

GEORGE/GEORGINA. What next?

RILEY. The show must...

Beat.

GEORGE/GEORGINA. Go on?
Forget?
Keep going, no matter what?

RILEY. Not forget, no,
but there's nothing for us here.

Beat.

It won't be the same.
But the story's the thing.
And I still have those.

Beat.

We'll be alright.
In these times people will always want what we have to
offer.

GEORGE/GEORGINA. What's that?

RILEY. Hope.

GEORGE/GEORGINA. Hope?
Hope?

RILEY. We are suing the doctor.
We are doing everything we can.
Tiny and Marketa understand that.
They know I never meant...

GEORGE/GEORGINA. Stop talking.
Please stop.
Not a townie.
Can't sell me a line.

RILEY *doesn't say anything*.

And Lillie?

RILEY. Why don't you ask her?

Beat.

She's not talking just yet.
But I thought maybe to you...

LILLIE*'s hand moves up and down, feeling the air beside her where* MILLIE *used to be.*

GEORGE/GEORGINA. How long will you carry her for?

RILEY. I don't intend on carrying her.

GEORGE/GEORGINA. You don't think she can still show?

RILEY. Perhaps.
When she's feeling better, of course.
I mean, one sister did survive.
There might be something in that.

Beat.

Mistakes were made.
Absolutely.
I acknowledge that.
I trusted where I shouldn't have.
And I was distracted when I shouldn't have been.
And yes.
Tragedy.
Real tragedy.

Beat.

But.
If,
When,
Lillie recovers
I am sure she will want to be with family.
And do what she knows.
And yes, show.
Her story, though heartbreaking, could also
In time
Not now of course

But eventually
Be seen in a positive light
As something she has survived, and grown through
And overcome
I think there's potential in that.
Townies do love that kind of story.

Pause.

GEORGE/GEORGINA. Would like to put you in a tank.
Would cut you to make half of you fat, and half of you thin,
half of you male and half of you female
half of you human and half of you creature
half of you hairy and half of you skin.
In a tank, up to your neck in water.
If you performed well might throw you a fish.
Would travel from place to place
Call out for everyone to come and see the most hideous
monster ever created.
There would be picture postcards to take away but they
wouldn't sell.
Children would run away crying,
Women would faint
Men would have nightmares.
Three shows a day.
I wouldn't charge.
No, not at all.
A public service.
You would be denounced from the pulpit
The medics would want you locked up.
And when the world had grown tired of you I would attach a
weight to your feet and sell tickets for the privilege of
watching you drown.

RILEY. Where will you go?

GEORGE/GEORGINA. I don't know.

RILEY. What will you do?
Remember:
You said yourself
'Can't ever just be one thing or another?'

GEORGE/GEORGINA *doesn't respond. They are beginning to change.*

RILEY. It seems to me that you're acting rashly.

Without a plan.

And out of grief.

I understand your anger.

GEORGE/GEORGINA. You don't.

You feel nothing.

You see us as belongings.

Millie.

Me.

As part of you.

An extra pair of hands to light the fires and hammer the pegs and sweep the floors and mend the wagon and show my strangeness.

But never your equal.

Never your colleague.

Never your friend.

MARKETA (*to* RILEY). I'm going.

There's no point in this.

(*To* GEORGE/GEORGINA.) Take care.

TINY. Good luck, I guess.

RILEY. You are on your own then.

RILEY *gives* GEORGE/GEORGINA *their case.* RILEY, MARKETA, TINY *and* LILLIE *exit.* TINY *pushes* LILLIE's *chair.*

G *stands up slowly, uncertainly. They look around the remains of the camp and find a mixture of male and female clothing. Slowly, deliberately, and with increasing confidence, G puts these new clothes on. They can put on make-up if that feels right. Sounds of modern life appear and grow in the background. There might be music. The house lights come up. G looks at us, and we see G. There is some hope.*

Blackout.

The End.